NO ORDINARY HOOK UP

THE COURTSHIP OF VASHTI TURLEY AND CARL MURPHY
1915-1916

By
Frances Murphy Draper

Published by Murphy Draper Publishing
Baltimore, Maryland

NO ORDINARY HOOK UP
THE COURTSHIP OF VASHTI TURLEY AND CARL MURPHY
1915-1916

Printed in the United States by CreateSpace
All rights reserved. The letters are the personal property of the author. This book or parts thereof may not be reproduced in any form, stored or transmitted by electronic, photocopy of other means without prior permission from the author.

ISBN-13: 978-1537047669
ISBN-10: 1537047663

2016 Copyright pending
Cover Design by: Gregory Johnson, Dominion Graphix
Edited by: Erica E. Campbell

Published by Murphy Draper Publishing
Baltimore, Maryland 21214

Photo (at the bottom of the cover) was taken August 7, 1959 at the Morgan Park home of Vashti Turley and Carl Murphy in Baltimore, MD. It is reportedly the last photo that they took together, before her death on March 17, 1960.

CONTENTS

Dedication..iv
Acknowledgements..v
Foreword...vii
Introduction..ix
"Dear Mr. Murphy…"..1
"Dear Miss Turley…"..7
"For You Alone"...13
"One Try Does Not Make a Fish"................................19
Tuesday, A Holy Day: Love Declared..........................29
"Better Luck Next Time"...35
"Of Course You May Come Over"..............................39
"Counting The Cost"...45
"I Loved You Before I Told You"................................51
The Wedding..57
12 Principles of Courtship..61
About Vashti Turley Murphy......................................63
About Carl Murphy...69
Grandchildren Remembrances....................................75
About The Author...79
Sampling of Original Letters......................................81

DEDICATION

To my husband, Mr. André Reginald Draper,
thank you for more than 40 years of love
and happiness. You are a wonderful example of what
it means to be a godly husband and a strong father
(and grandfather). May our marriage, built on Christian
principles, continue to inspire other couples
to "love and to cherish till death do us part".

ACKNOWLEDGEMENTS

To God be the glory for the great things He has done. First of all, I thank my Lord and Savior Jesus Christ for inspiring me to write this book. Second, I thank my grandparents Carl and Vashti Murphy for leaving a written legacy of their courtship and for teaching us about love, marriage, family, sacrifice and service. Third, I am grateful to my cousins and my brother for sharing their remembrances of our grandparents. Last, but not least, I thank my friends Drs. Pam Love Manning and Surina Ann Jordan for their coaching and encouragement; Gregory Johnson for designing the cover; Erica Campbell for her editing assistance; and, the Rev. Nicole D. Batey for helping to format this book. Prayerfully, these letters will encourage couples, especially young couples, to contend for a God-centered, long-lasting relationship that goes way beyond an "ordinary hook up".

FOREWORD

My grandparents, Vashti and Carl Murphy, were very prim and proper when we were growing up in our own homes and at the dinner table on Overland Avenue. I do not remember a time when they held hands in front of us or stole a kiss over the soup in the kitchen when we weren't looking. There were a lot of long looks across the table and quiet smiles. Of course, as children we had no idea what the looks and smiles meant. They had a deep respect for each other. There was also a quiet intimacy and companionship that edged their love for one another. He ran a newspaper. She ran a house. But a lot of the energetic creativity and social justice commitment began as pillow talk. How that all developed in an age where courtship consisted of an invitation to an afternoon tea, a chaperoned lunch or a series of letters is beyond the 21st century imagination. Love bloomed in between formal honorifics, conservative conversation and decorum.

My cousin Rev. Dr. Frances Murphy Draper captures their courtship through their letters to remind us of a time where extraordinary hookups emerged out of ordinary literary exchanges. Enjoy!

~ Bishop Vashti Murphy McKenzie

Bishop McKenzie serves as the 117th elected and consecrated bishop of the African Methodist Episcopal (AME) Church. Her historic election in the year 2000 represents the first time in the over 200-year history of the AME Church a woman obtained the level of Episcopal office. Currently, she is honored to serve as the presiding prelate of the 10th Episcopal District, which is the entire state of Texas. She is the oldest granddaughter of Carl and Vashti Turley Murphy's 16 grandchildren. For over 40 years, Bishop McKenzie has been married to Stan McKenzie. They have three children and one granddaughter.

INTRODUCTION

The rise of "hook ups", a form of casual sex, has been described by evolutionary biologist, Justin Garcia, as a "cultural revolution" that had its beginnings in the 1920s. Technological advancements such as the automobile and movie theaters brought young couples out of their parents' homes and away from their watchful eyes, giving young people more freedom and more opportunity for sexual activity.

With the loosening sexual morals that came with the sexual revolution in the 1960s, sex became uncoupled from relationships and non-marital sex became more socially accepted. Some scholars, including Garcia, have found that while dating has not disappeared, it has decreased as hook up culture has become more common. By the mid-1990s, hook ups were an accepted form of relating among sexually active adults, especially on college campuses.

One hundred years ago, young people also had a desire to "hook up", but the connotation was completely different than it is today. A hook up was not about casual sex, but was the precursor to a lifetime commitment—a "for better, for worse, for richer, for poorer, in sickness and in health, to love and to cherish, till death do us part, according to God's holy ordinances; and thereto I pledge thee my faith"--kind of commitment. And, in preparation for this lifetime commitment, this "dating" period was called a courtship. One online dictionary defines "courtship" as "a period during which a couple develops a romantic relationship, especially with a view to marriage".

In 1911, my grandparents, Carl Murphy and Lula Vashti Turley (known by her middle name) "hooked up" at Howard University in Washington, D.C. – he, the German professor, and she, the German student; he, born in 1889, and she, five years earlier (see bios at the end of the book); he, the Alpha Phi Alpha man, and she, one of the 22 founders of Delta Sigma Theta Sorority, Inc.; he, the editor of the AFRO-American Newspaper founded by his father in 1892 and she, the D.C. school teacher; she, the only survivor of her immediate family who all died from a plague, he one of ten children—five boys and five girls. It wasn't until after she was graduated from Howard in 1913 that she invited the young professor "to call". But this was no ordinary hook up!

It was a courtship extraordinaire—a relationship based on a strong faith in God, on who they were as individuals, as well as on who they hoped to become as a couple. The letters that follow cover a seven-month period (February, 1915- September, 1915) and discuss a variety of topics such as religion, literature, theater, politics, social justice, civil rights, music and, of course, love. There are some gaps in the dates of the letters so the reader is invited to let your imagination (especially your romantic side) fill in the blanks. Carl James Greenbury Murphy and Lula Vashti Turley were married on Tuesday, June 20, 1916. They were married for 43 years, until her death on March 17, 1960.

The issue of marriage stability and sustainability is one of particular interest to me. As a pastor, I am often called upon to perform weddings, yet, I also receive many calls from couples whose marriages are in trouble. Unfortunately, too many couples spend more time on wedding preparations than they do on preparing for healthy, stable, long-lasting, and satisfying marriages. As a result, I have spent more than twenty-five years researching, teaching, and advising on the value of premarital counseling as a necessary precursor to marriage. In doing so, I reflect not only on the theoretical or the theological (while both are important), but also on the practical and historical.

I vividly remember the weekly trips to my grandparents' home in Morgan Park and how wonderful it was to see them interact with each other. My own parents were divorced, so my brother, sister, and I did not have a father in the home. We were around a lot of other married couples, but none were like our grandparents. While our grandparents seldom hugged or kissed publicly, even amongst family, they had a deep and abiding respect for each other. My five-foot, two-inch tall grandfather, by all accounts, could be a tyrant, but you could always count on him to respond "yes, dear" when my grandmother softly reminded him that while he was in charge of the AFRO (the AFRO-American Newspaper), she was in charge of the house.

Their marriage was an extension of their courtship. As a married couple, they continued to read and passionately discuss a variety of books, listen to good music (grandfather was a huge fan of German operas), and fellowship with people of all races and cultures. They also loved and cherished family time, as well as family ties. Building a long-lasting, trusting relationship was important. So was attending church at St. James Episcopal as a family, and serving their community.

Their courtship and marriage served as one of the frameworks for my doctoral thesis, "Relationship Theology: A Model for Producing Healthy Marriages in the African American Context". I am convinced that what happens before couples say "I do" determines the quality and length of their marriage. Even though Carl and Vashti Murphy "courted" and married over 100 years ago, the principles that they embraced are still relevant today. It was no ordinary hook up!

Author's Note: For the most part, the letters are transcribed exactly as written in an attempt to maintain the authentic spelling and grammar of the early 1900's. In addition, the reader will note that their salutations quickly progressed from "Dear Mr. Murphy, Dear Miss Turley" to "Dear Vashti, Dear Carl"---from an intellectual courtship to an intimate declaration of love.

"Dear Mr. Murphy..."

1914 3rd St.
Washington D.C.
Feb. 2, 1915

I regret very much to hear of your mother's continued illness but hope that some improvement will be noticed soon.

Mrs. Booth wishes to be especially remembered to your Sister.

L. Vashti Turley

At School - March 24, 1915

Dear Mr. Murphy,

I was just a little surprised at the feeling you expressed in your note. I thoroughly realized that you stayed with us only after you were urged to do so by both Mrs. Booth and me. We all enjoyed having you.

Unfortunately I have a very full program this week but will be at home on Sunday, as usual. If you need your diary, you can call or send anytime.

March 30, 1915

Dear Mr. Murphy,

I realize that I owe you an apology for this long delay in acknowledging the music. Need I say, or can I say, how much I appreciate your kindness?

I had really forgotten that last week was your week for going home. Nevertheless, I hope to be able to thank you in person soon.

Sincerely,
L. Vashti Turley

Washington, D.C.
April 14, 1915

Dear Mr. Murphy,

Your letter came just in time to prevent me from sending out detectives. Seriously though anytime will do for the "debt."

It is very kind of you to invite me to see the play Saturday. I shall be delighted.

Sincerely,
L. Vashti Turley

The paper is the very best I can find in the house tonight.

5/1/15

Dear Mr. Murphy,

Over the phone this morning, Miss Fairfax Brown invited me to come to her house tonight for an informal affair. (Hate to name it.) If you are free will you accompany me?

Hope this reaches you in time.

Sincerely,

L. V. Turley

6/15/15

Dear Mr. Murphy,

It isn't quite 5:30 a.m., but don't wonder at it. I got up for a game, thinking the ground would surely be ready after yesterday's heat, but I am truly disappointed.

I finished "Redder Blood" last week. Will tell you what I think of it when I see you. I am just beginning to enjoy O. Henry.

Thanks for the pamphlets. Truly, though I think not only pupils would show what they do not know but teachers also. I wouldn't want any witnesses when being tested. Mr. Thomas, of the Normal School, gave a talk on the tests to groups of teachers, consisting of one from each building, recently. They found it very interesting.

Do you remember my telling you of an article on Cook's "Exhortation."? I inquired and the informer thinks it is in the "Christian Work" for April. You might run across it.

L. Vashti Turley

June 15, 1915 – I had to open this. I had addressed the envelope with 937 Girard Street, Baltimore, Md. and suddenly the strangeness of it flashed across my mind. Last week I wrote you a note and I'm wondering if I did the same thing. Please drop me a card and tell me if you got it. I wrote it on Tues. Can't find your home address. Yes, I realize just how senseless such a stunt is.

Dear Mr. Murphy,

Glad to know that your group has really done a little more than plan and hope some real work will be done. Will be glad to see you when you enter civilization.

6/23/15

Sincerely,
L. Vashti Turley

6/30/15

Dear Mr. Murphy,

I was so sorry when Mr. Edmunds came that I was forced to let him go before reading your note. I haven't forgot what I have in store for him and I think the longer I reserve it the greater I will have to make it appear.

Shall be at home and will be the usual to see you. At least give me credit that the phraseology is original. Thanks.

Sincerely,
L Vashti Turley

"Dear Miss Turley..."

July 3, 1915

Carl J. Murphy
Howard University
Washington, D.C.

Concerning a very reluctantly loaned diary:

If I have laughed at anything, it was a certain fish dinner where some people had clam chowder and gutters, steamed and fried clams etc. etc. One could well wonder that there were no roast or missed clams, no clam broth or pot-pie, and need not wonder that a later entry speaks of a "rejected lobster."

I remember, tho, if I am "good", perhaps may hear about the "autocrat at the breakfast table" and his traipse thru Boston Commons.

In your visit to the state house, I do not see that you mention the Shaw Monument, directly opposite.

Did you feel as I did about the mural paintings of the Holy Grail in Boston library? It is to be deplored that they are not in a gallery but high up on the walls of a public building, compressed by the natural limitations of that single room and the necessity of the paintings occupying the whole space, distorted by projections of windows, doors and shelving, as I remember, and finally so placed that good lighting do not allow us to do full justice, even with the help of excellent card explanations furnished by the library.

Not being in the position of the man about to be hanged, we can save some good things for the morrow.
With some expectancy we think of (your account of) Niagara Falls which we have often seen but never heard.

C. J. M.

Howard University
Washington, D.C.

Dear Miss Turley,

I have just come from a stormy interview with the director of the Hopkins Summer School. We were nearly to the point of saying, "can't" and "can" to each other. He was obdurate, however I insisted, maintaining virtually that all men are not created equal, and they celebrate too today the anniversary of the ratification of the Declaration of Independence, this afternoon with community singing and games, tonight with fireworks. For our people it seems they are putting in– better half a country than no native land. I can't feel they are right.

Doctor was kind enough to ask me back to camp today. I promised to think about it. Remembering your advice tho, I am sending Wesley back alone.

Your diary is in the post, without a four-leafed clover, with some music, which I trust you are going to like. "Dawn" seems a simple melody with much of its charm in the accompaniment. I believe we have heard it together. "For you alone" I did not select because Coruso is said to have sung it.

And now for DuBois "The Negro". Until now the critics have kept quiet. They appear to be waiting for someone to find something especially praise or blameworthy before they begin a tirade. Dean Miller thinks the book a compilation of quoted facts and represents little that is original, admits tho the chapter on the 'Slave Trade" to be the big part of the book. One does miss the kind of imagination in DuBois history that paints pictures: pictures like Green's description of Queen Elisabeth or Carlyle's description of the king on the way to execution in the "French Revolution".

What one does get, and that is worth more is the Negro in another historical light. From the earliest migrations into Africa from Asia down to the 15th Century, including the civilizations of the Babylonians Egyptians and some others, DuBois says Africa was abreast or in advance of Europe. With the coming of the slave traders she was dispirited to the point of degeneration, retarded beyond ability to catch up in the last four centuries. With it all the African is not more nor less than intensely human, undoubtedly not inherently backward. In the past century DuBois' summaries of causes and results of movements illuminates after fifty years of hypocrisy!

The civil war was fought to segregate slavery not to abolish it; the Negros' need of immediate education and his control of the government during reconstruction are first causes of the rise of the public school system in the South; present poverty of the Negro is due to the failure of the government to make some payment for 250 years of slavery and free labor. These things not in the common histories, he thinks worth knowing and strives to popularize by sending forth "The Negro" in a fifty-cent edition.

The plan of the book is extremely simple. Africa is divided in five geographical sections and the history of each brought down to the present day—this one half the book. The second half, not one chapter, deals with the Negro in the New World, beginning with the arrival of slaves and concluding with a forecast of the future. The one chapter connecting the Old and the New Worlds is the one I have mentioned – "The Trade in Men."

This was the subject of his doctor's thesis at Harvard and is characteristically DuBoisians in contrasts and bitterness. You can't help feeling with him the cruel inhumanity that devastated all Africa and carried away one hundred million as slaves.

And we think that Europe too would have been a "dark continent" had she suffered likewise. And this he concludes went on for four hundred years, while Luther preached, Raphael painted, and Milton wrote, "Such is the story of the rape of Ethiopia," who during four centuries stretched forth her hands unto God."

You may recall that Dubois is (an) AΦA man. He told us some six years ago that there are many facts in Negro history doomed to remain hidden, unless we develop Negro historians. He seemed to have realized that the best way to get a thing done___ ___ ___. Above all things he emphasizes as he always does that this race is ancient of ancients, a fallen hero and not a swaddling infant. Trust you had a bang up trip.

Very Truly,
Carl J. Murphy

July 5, 1915

Written from Baltimore 1320 D.H. (Druid Hill) Ave.

"For You Alone"

Washington, D.C.
July 6, 1915

Dear Mr. Murphy,

I must admit that my first day home was made quite interesting, all due to you. I first read the comment on the diary. I reread parts of it (diary) and lived over some experiences. I had to agree with you about the Holy Grail paintings but confess that at the time I simply accepted the condition as a matter of course. Another confession is that I've forgot what Miss Lewis told me about the walk. Think it is something I must look up for myself. Please don't pass judgment.

The music is a real treat. I have enjoyed both pieces today.

I really believe you chose "For You Alone" because of the simplicity of the cover and the "Birth of Morn" because of recent early rising. It matters not about the reason, I shall enjoy them both and try hard to play them well enough for you to recognize them when you come over.

After reading later in the day the summary of "The Negro" I couldn't forget, try as hard as I might my promise. So I shall try to summarize "Redder Blood" though I fear I shan't be as pleased with my result as I am with yours.

July 7, 1915

Last night I reached the above place and just couldn't exert will power sufficient to continue. It was due no doubt to the long ride after effects.

"Redder Blood" is an interesting story in which the author takes an old theme and dares to prove his foreword "that neither custom nor convention nor law are great enough barriers to keep two persons apart (who love deeply)."

His characterization of the American white man who talks about abiding by the "laws of nature, justice and God" when he really isn't called upon to do anything, is good. His man raves when he realizes his wife has Negro blood but unlike the "New Governor" his character is strong enough not to be ruled by convention. If only a white author would dare!

Of course we recognize that, as the only true attitude and hope the day will soon come when it will be universal. The author attempts further on to break down another convention, but failed to relish it.

To me, it is a touch that spoils the book. He makes the girl Wanda a suitor to the man Adrian. He places all of the initiative on her which to me weakens both of the characters. And yet that is what he starts out to prove.

To the first (race) case I say "Amen," to the second, there is too much prominence given to this part of the story anyway. That is the way I felt first but now this afterthought makes me see that the author has endowed the white woman with "redder blood" which compels her to act as did the white man and such a method was probably necessary. I started off to write as though you knew the story; which I suppose you do. For fear you don't, here is a synopsis.

Mr. Birch, a prominent and wealthy young man meets with an accident and is carried to a hospital. He falls in love with his nurse and marries her. Their years pass by happily and their son proves himself worthy of their love.

All goes well until a new manservant comes into the house as chef. He turns out to be the one man who knows Mrs. Birch's life history. She is of Negro descent. He tries to force her away with him and threatens to expose her. He uses many methods to get her away from her home but each time is thwarted.

One morning her husband and son return home and surprise the man forcibly seizing Mrs. Birch. It is then that her husband learns the truth. He leaves home quietly not intending that anyone shall know that he has left for good. The son who is twenty-two and engaged immediately hastens to break his engagement, but the girl after her first display of anger and disgust decides color is no barrier. Later the father returns for the same reason.

The author touches many social questions and sends forth an ideal point of view of some.

_____FINIS_____

Had a delightful time on the Bay. The water was fine and there was quite an agreeable bunch of people. Unfortunately, we had tire trouble both ways. Otherwise the ride was lovely. We went through Baltimore going over but came back by Marlborough, which is a more delightful and shorter ride.

If one could just chase away the mosquitoes all would be well.

I tried to learn to take a stroke in the water but alas, I always went to the bottom until I finally gave up in disgust.

Went out this morning for a game of tennis. Had a nice game of hot red "pepper."

I fully appreciated how you must have felt after your recent interview but at any rate I'll wager you gave him just a little food for thought. I suppose after all, we've got hope that something <u>must</u> happen soon.

    I'm afraid I regret giving that unasked for advice but will know better in the future.

Sincerely,
L. Vashti Turley

The sweater was a necessity and don't know how I would have got on without it. <u>Thanks again.</u>

"One Try Does Not Make a Fish"

Howard University
Washington, D.C.

Dear Miss Turley,

Have *(you)* seen the reflection of yourself in "God was Outdoors"? Of course it was no little boy at all "playing hookey" from an afternoon Sunday School, but a very grown girl, who rebelled at church after Sunday School and sometimes at both services and avoided the minister rather than confess that there was more inspiration in open temples, than in a stuffy church.

She did not foresee that, what she hesitated to say about morning services might with justification be said of afternoon services and in this very orthodox community, orthodox to the point of fanaticism becomes the basis of an argument to abridge Sunday exercises.

As if this were not enough, the call of the outdoors is identified with the instinct to worship and the impulse to reverence. How much haven't you to answer for besides rebellion? In the end is it the call of nature or it is youth that will be served, and if it is the former as we usually put it, why does it not come to the elders and make argument and persuasion unnecessary? As if you were right, my Sunday School next door sings prayerfully "God be with us <u>here</u> today."

I have chanced upon a new Negro composer, Anderson. His "If You Forget" is said to be worthwhile by western critics. Do you know anything that he has done? I can't say a word about the title lest I begin to apologize as you did.

Your "It matters not about the reason" takes away for the future any incipient hesitancy. And too, speaking of music, I admit I am right about the unusualness of the ending in "Nobody at Home".

I am glad of your review of Mr. Ashby's effort. You make it plain that he combats two conventions in that he argues for intermarriage and equality of sexes. I note your "Amen" to the first because you recognize in this the only true attitude where sentiment exists between white and black people and your "Never" to the second unsupported by any reason, axiomatic.

So be sure the training of this generation has been that self-assertion for women may not be carried beyond a certain point under pain of calling forth the epithet <u>forward</u> or <u>unwomanly</u>. In another age it was unwomanly if one held an opinion contrary to that of one's parents. Today it is unwomanly not to think for one's self and to express that individual judgment both publicly and privately except – in the matter of sentiment.

Initiative in voting for example is perfectly in order, but in questions of "feeling," you are not to be trusted.

It would be a splendid thing if the women of the other race would say "Amen" to your "Amen." In the question of intermarriage they would feel just and reason only to find justification, so that they would conclude never to your "Amen," and very probably "Amen" to your "Never," where reason and logic admit but one conclusion.

To bring it closer, you argue the just question because it is not near enough to affect you personally --- to be felt and express a decided opinion on the second based on feeling alone which is here regarded argument sufficient.

So the rebel has become reactionary. Your intuition of the proper place of woman in this generation is undoubtedly correct, but in the future, you who pursue suffrage, simple moral standard and, in general, equality, must come to the place where they do not recognize womanly women and manly men, but simply people.

I expect you have heard how ingloriously our tennis team was beaten last Saturday. I have not been able to explain to them yet why I would not go.

It's kind of you to regret your advice, unkind to advise and then regret. I have been afraid that you would run away to an inaccessible "Porchville" and never come back. Won't you then arrange our picnic for the first of August or thereabout? By then I can think of another vacation.

>Very truly yours,
>Carl J. Murphy
>Baltimore, MD
>July 11. 1915

P.S. One try does not make a fish.

Washington, D.C.
July 13, 1915

Dear Mr. Murphy,

Before I received your letter, I was suspicious of the identity of the editor of "God is Outdoors" and now my suspicions are confirmed. I am still in the rebellious mood and find the call of the open too strong to resist. While at Arundel my attention left the beauty of the trees and centered on the voice of the ocean. My imagination couldn't interpret the language very well but at any rate there was something.

For the pleasure and benefit of a next match (a thing I hadn't dared hope for) I'll furnish a <u>whole</u> cabbage if necessary.

Will you be surprised to know that I've changed my plans just a little? I've decided to spend a short while at Annapolis leaving home either Thursday night or Friday morning. Of course, I'll go to Arundel for a few days. I will be home the last week in July and the early part of August.

I'm in for the picnic anytime that you can come. In August I've decided to spend about a week at the Ferry. So that will alter our plans for picnic, no. 2, though you could decide to take a week-end instead of a Sunday. You'd better think about it.

I haven't seen Harriet since the match but will consult with her about stunt no.1 and let you know.

I cut this clipping out of Saturday's "Star" and thought it might interest you.

I had almost forgot the music. The last piece doesn't serve as evidence at all. The whys I will have to give you verbally. Man's use of that argument has become hackneyed and I'm really surprised at you using it. Of course I know it was simply a joke with you but it is appalling to think how many men use it seriously.
Don't want to forget to thank you for "Fake-Literary News."

After Thursday, I will be at 80 Franklin Street, Annapolis, Md.

Sincerely,

L. Vashti Turley

Have you reached "A Far Country" yet? Will comment on your P.S. when I see you. "I think it is", Miss Parm would say.

Howard University

Washington, D.C.

Dear Miss Turley,

I was interrupted before I started this – if that is possible. Next door, an evangelist of whom the town is beginning to talk, began and continued an exhortation so loudly that the curious was attracted. After three-quarters of an hour of billy sundaying, he found an unresponsive audience and no one who wanted to be saved. He says, tho, he is determined -- "at the end of the week I am going to have five hundred converts even if all hell is against me," and further if sinners do not respond I'll "marshal forces in the street and sing and shout all over Baltimore."

It's a sin to dance, to play ragtime and to play cards. I was interested to hear his reason… "would you like to die doing any one of these three things" – congregation "no" --- Billy Sunday, "then it is a sin to do in life, what you would not like to die doing."

I had finished your "A Far Country" some four hours before your call this morning. The atmosphere of the conflict of business and ethics that Churchill presents and the haze from the land of mind lingered so that the recognition of your voice came out slowly. I expect it is "hackneyed" to say I was glad to hear you. I have seen Arundel in everything since I wandered from the sermon this morning and felt certain the gilt letters on the altar piece spelled something like your swimming resort. Please may I may come down for an afternoon this week? Will call you up tomorrow.

Of course I liked the book, so well that I finished it immediately. It must be read again before I can say I appreciate bravery and the romantic part of the individualistic hero. In the theory of reeducation I concur, it bolsters my own – that democracy is a failure in America.

The effort of his to reconcile religion and business methods is clear enough, the examples showing the need of such reconciliation are splendidly worked out, but the conclusion, his scientific religion, what it is and how operative, is suggestive but not convincing. The way you state your own problem, his manner of presenting his, both make me feel uncanny. The way you put your fingers on things leads me to wonder just what assurance it is I have missed. When it comes finally to my evangelist, I can't think he is sincere.

This "Two Sails" is one of the simpler things Conrad Ferdinand Meyer has done. I believe we read something of his, perhaps "The Amulet" last year. I have lost a foot in one verse and am guilty of a repetition in one stanza – I can't think of two other words. It's typical of the kind of imagination most of his poems show:

Two Sails

Two white sails brightening
The dark blue sky
Two white sails fast swelling
To fly far away.
As one with the brisk wind bends and moves forward.
Then too is the mind of the other accordant.
Doth one wish hastening
The other doth lend
Doth one desire resting
Rests to then his friend.

Some perfect days may be produced at will. We may not be able to summon perfect weather to suit our convenience, but we need not mind the weather if it is inclement.

Very truly yours,
Carl Murphy

July 18, 1915 Baltimore, 1320 D.H. Ave. (The church is Bethel)

7/31/'15

Dear Mr. Murphy,

If I had followed out my intention, I would have written you a note earlier in the week. I too was sorry when I learned I had missed you in Annapolis. My stay in Arundel was delightful and I <u>almost</u> swam. (I hope some day to be able to get away from that almost word.)

Thanks for the paper and magazine. I will have a tiny something to be said about the marked copy. It will sound better than it looks so wait until next week. Now, don't tremble, the worst is yet to come.

I suppose the others will be willing to plan for next week. Haven't seen anyone. Come anyway.

Sincerely,

L.V.T.

Tuesday, A Holy Day: Love Declared

Carl J. Murphy
Howard University
Washington, D.C.

Dear Vashti,

The full realization of what Tuesday has meant can come but slowly. To be sure I did not understand then and there comes moments when I wonder do I yet understand—is it true that you do love me and have promised to be my wife. Even now I comprehend my impatience that so nearly approached thotlessness, and kept you out far later than you should have stayed; for you should have time to think.

Think now, dear, nor "answer" until restraining doubts can be put aside to make it fully free, and think of the love I offer as more of worship and of reverence. There is nothing higher in my life.

Faithfully yours,
Carl

P.S. Shall write you Sunday.
August 12, 1915   Written from Baltimore 1320 Druid Hill Ave.

August 13, 1915 –

Washington D.C.

Dear Carl,

I did not know how anxiously I was awaiting your letter until I received it, and in like manner I did not dream what the declaration of your love would mean to me until it came. To describe all that I felt then is impossible. I only know that since Tuesday I have realized that I do care.

This is simply an assurance that it is all true and I felt that I must tell you. Forgive my hesitancy and believe that I want to be genuine.

Sincerely,

Vashti

August, 1915

Love poem to Vashti:

The God in Me

You love me then because my eyes are bright?
Old age will come and hide from them the light.
You love me then because my face is fair?
The years will pass and press the wrinkles there.
You love me then for I am straight and strong?
Bowed down with cares I yet may walk along,
Beauty will fade, but not the God in me,
Love that, beloved, to eternity.

August 15, 1915

To Vashti,

The darkness falls, alone I sit at ease
The church bells send their message far and wide,
Light fancies linger in the evening breeze,
I dream of other days at eventide---
A longed-for face, a gently whispered name
Thou heart of my heart, heart's very own?
My arms stretch out for thee---in vain, I face the coming of the night alone.

Carl J. Murphy
Howard University
Washington, D.C.

Dear Vashti,

This explains what I was doing before coming indoors to write you this. Church did not offer much this morning, and I went to two: perhaps you would put it that I did not carry anything to them. This church I have just had tho -- the one in my yard, where I have been thinking of you – has been splendid. The text of the dream minister was, "see thou to the four-leafed clover – for it shall bring good fortune." And for a hymn, "Blessed Assurance." Tuesday was declared holy day above all others, until with the years it be supplanted by one other still more significant; and confession decreed for the very next day that we meet.

I thot of you in selecting "Cheer Up" from the exchanges of the week. It embodied so perfectly the philosophy you spoke of, that is yours. My life has evolved (*into*) one that is different. Temperament and training have accustomed it to a harsher and sterner view of things. Your sweetness and light will make smooth the rough places and make real our make believes.

Schooled you have termed yourself, which is being interpreted---to find pleasure in doing things in but one way— your way. Together we shall think of one thing alone---the best way; in your philosophy lies the place of salvation, and the question is only – if we will. I find myself preaching and I did not mean to, even though it is Sunday. Shall send you pictures in the morning.

Until then,
Dein Dich liebender
(*Loving you*)
Carl

August 15, 1915

"Better Luck Next Time"

Carl J. Murphy
Howard University
Washington, D.C.

Dear Vashti,

Because I wanted all five pictures of you to turn out well, only one of them did. Possibly you will think I believe you now---that you don't take a good picture---but I don't. The fault lies in the fact that we did not have sunlight enough. I'm the one on the rock, you moved slightly, but the one sitting in your yard—the serious one, had the promise of being excellent. Better luck next time.

Meantime, I shan't feel quite so disappointed if you send me one of yourself.

Yours,

August 16, 1915   Carl

Tuesday   August 17, 1915 – Washington D.C.

Dear Carl,

    At this moment I'm enjoying the prettiest, "smelliest" pink rosebud that I've seen this summer. Would that I could share it with you, (had been to McWilliam's Park Reservoir), to hear the Marine Band and the rose came as a fitting finale to a pleasant evening. The concert was exceptionally fine but I couldn't enjoy it to the fullest for two reasons – one, I didn't have foresight enough to carry a wrap and was cold; the other sounds something like being lonesome in a big crowd.

    I don't know what is wrong with the collection of mail in Baltimore, but I do know that I received both of your letters this morning. The first one had two stampings 10:00 a.m. and 1:30 p.m. I should have received it Monday evening.

    It's too bad about the pictures but don't be disappointed please. Remember the ones you took on the River. They were good. Let's don't talk about pictures for a long, long time.

    Will you be surprised when I tell you that I went to church Sunday too? Jr. Washington of the Social Settlement spoke on "Ye are the salt of the earth etc." I came home pleased and helped, but on receiving your letter this morning I rather thought that I might have been helped by attending your church.

    The "Master of the Inn" is a beautiful little sketch full of food for thought. I found very much to apply to myself and hope

– need I say it? Don't you anticipate that I hope for the power to "forget and be new" in a new world with you.

Find that I can't get away until September. Was negligent of some business earlier, and now find I'm compelled to stay.

Mrs. Norwood is in Atlantic City and writes me that she doesn't know how long she'll remain. So I'm not likely to be in Annapolis again for some time.

We're having ideal weather for stay-at homes so should not complain. When I read the Athletic news, I wasn't surprised at a certain C.J.M's rating, but I was impressed anew of his generosity, and patience in playing with a certain beginner. I'll save the rest, I would say until…

Sincerely,

Vashti

J.H. N. Waring, Lydia Brown, and Vashti Turley (Ma).

Rose Norwood, The Annapolis Matchmaker.

"Of Course You May Come Over"

Howard University

Washington, D.C.

Dear Vashti,

I have thot terrible things of a post-office system that takes more than a day to bring you my letter. Someone was kind enough this last time to reseal your envelope, so it can't be thoroly bad.

The group on the river could not have been forgotten, nor the class book of your year with its photos and history. This with your "please" nearly convince me that I am not disappointed. But I am.

Speaking of "Nikh" reminds me that it chronicles the fact that you "will continue to teach in the Washington Public Schools." It does not suggest what until further on, where the subject "Tango" recurs.

I am flattered by the nice things you say about our tennis, (*I*) don't however deserve any special credit. You see I love to begin things with you any way, and there is the big beginning that we have yet to make. I have had two matches this week, both of which went to the fifth set before I could win three. The result is one position higher.

Author's Note: "Nikh" is the name of a 1915 Howard University Yearbook.

A party had been planned to carry a match to Annapolis on Wednesday and I had expected remotely to convey, to little Vashti that Auntie has reluctantly adopted me. The auto broke down at the last minute and with sour grapes philosophy---your letter notes that the Norwoods are away.

The playground has been the real subject of the week. The centers close next week, so that I have been occupied getting a summary of their work written and pictures of the various grounds. This last frequently entailed telling the play director that it was not hers but the children's picture that the office wanted.

Until now I have been interested simply in playground work. There is something pathetic in the poverty of the smaller charges, and their hero-worship of the director, and in the realization of the inadequacy of this institution alone to cope with crime prevention. The fact obtrudes itself—if the forces for good are not in the home, school nor playground can help much. They do help but it is poor compensation that takes money out of wages and puts it into playground.

Since you are the putting off your trip until later, may I come over for a weekend on the 29th? I really want to come tomorrow, but the other is more sensible—you won't ask me then

why did I come to Washington.

Baltimore August 20, 1915

Truly yours,
Carl

August 22, 1915

Washington DC

Dear Carl,

No doubt it is commendable to be "sensible" but many times in the last few days I've wanted not to be, and wanted to ask you to come. You must have been conscious of some such idea. Of course, you may come over but do you realize that the 29th is Sunday --- or is that what you intended?

It isn't necessary to say that I read "Compensation" today. Are you sure, Carl, that you sent it because it "has been frequently mentioned of late"? I think it contains a wonderful, hopeful ideal philosophy. His is a point of view if we would live, we must eventually adapt.

When striving men, conscientious men see constant failures confronting them at every turn, they are inclined, it is only natural, on seeing their scheming neighbors apparently successful to wonder if there is to be justice meted out. But we are not to judge but to have faith in God's natural laws.

Mr. Emerson impresses me as believing that good is sure to triumph and that every set back in one's life is also a stepping stone to an ideal character. Is that what you get?

I didn't go to church this morning, but really think as much help was gathered from the reading.

The receipt of both "essays" and music made me very happy because I know you were thinking of me. Shall try the music tomorrow.

Have been reading V.V.'s Eyes by Harrison. Find he has quite a sane point of view on modern woman and hence, suffrage. He deals with factory life showing the ignorance of wealthy wives and daughters as to how their fortune is made at the expense of the poor. Will have to tell you more about it when I see you, if you haven't read it.

I forgot to tell you that I really liked your editorials this week. The one on "Religion" seemed to me just the right thing in a nutshell. No, don't accuse me of hero-worship: that's a perfectly impartial remark.

Sincerely (yours),
Vashti

"You ask if I love you is beautiful."

Carl J. Murphy
Howard University
Washington, D.C.

Dear Vashti,

"Honest Injun" I have not read Emerson's "Compensation." I thot the rain that set in Saturday might last over Sunday, keeping you indoors. With Emerson and the Sunday thot you had, then two sermons at home, I am happy in knowing that you were, a happiness increased only by the realization that you have given me the right to keep you so until the end of life.

From what I have heard about the essay, I expected something of the sort. Please mark some of the things you liked and save them for me. If his compensation means the same as retribution, I have always felt that punishment was here on earth not anywhere else; and the opposite, reward or heaven here. You remember the lines of Milton.

"The mind is its own place and itself can make a hell of heaven, a heaven of hell.

The ultimate triumph of the good reminds me of Carlyn's grain of sand – today in the desert of Sahara, tomorrow on the bed of the Indian Ocean – never lost and sure to give an account of itself at some time.

I am only wondering whether more emphasis is placed on the will of the individual not to judge for himself or on his faith in the operation of natural laws.

I told father of the last paragraph in your letter – your comment on "Shall we look for another religion?" He smiled. The heading is mine but the editorial is the only one he has condescended to write since he decided on a vacation. His smile must have been in appreciation of the "perfectly impartial remark."

You must know how hard I have found it to stay in Baltimore the last three weeks. Coming this week I may have a day longer – Saturday thru Monday.

I told Coach we might play tennis Saturday afternoon. Shall drop by for a minute early in the morning about eleven – I did mean the 28th rather than the 29th.

                                              Until then,

August 25, 1915   Carl

Baltimore, MD

"Counting The Cost"

Dear Carl,

Of course you must be the very first to receive a note. It was really lovely of you to think of me this way but I must confess that the appreciation is an afterthought. Why? Because of my anxiety to receive a letter. It wouldn't be extreme to say I was starving for one. But I finally ate my breakfast, swallowed the disappointment, and awakened the appreciation. Please don't laugh! It's rather hard getting back to anything systematic. Certainly enjoyed the vacation.

Have managed to read one chapter of Queed. By the way the author is Henry Sidney [Sydnor] Harrison. My chief character is again one of these strange personalities. This time a sociologist and a fanatic. Not that they go together. Looks like it will be interesting.

Vashti

September 2, 1915

Carl J. Murphy
Howard University
Washington, D.C.

Dear Vashti,

Do you remember that you wanted to write some things rather than say them and that just as before I urged the now? You were right a second time. We could accuse ourselves of sober thot only by waiting and thinking it thru. The new experience of finding you instantly overwhelmed anything that suggested a closing of the doors of the temple. Sensible now, but not then, was your idea of counting the cost before we became too happy.

"If one would only plan thru things like he plans his work"---on the back of your last letter I wrote the two words <u>health</u> and <u>income</u>. These two things we were going to talk about in our three days. I did not know how hard it should be to bring such material things into our new world. I know now I did not want to. We did not finish the first.

Are we modern, you have asked. I am not if it means I shall give you up because of the untimely death of the others in your family. You have not told me about all of them yet; not that it can change the complexion of affairs do I ask it, but I feel that you want me to know.

Today folk place emphasis, overemphasis, on the duty parents owe to their children that are to be. I believe we owe as much to ourselves.

If we, both of us, are physically and mentally sound, we need not consider what has been or what will be. Like the first couple we start with ourselves. Of our own strength and will, we may live nor allow specters of the past or future to frighten us.

This is the theory of our family physician – for intelligent people there is no danger. It remains for us not to think that we are beginning with a handicap or that either one of us concedes something here. Believe rather that your self-sufficiency begins here, working in all other things, where of I love you.

I comprehend what it means for you to go over this with someone outside of your immediate family. Churchill was not wrong in his view that sacredness attaches itself more to mutual consent than to a marriage ceremony. The first is this union of spirits and the second but the garment of custom. And this other thing lets him as always be frank, brutally frank even if necessary. Doubts too easily form a framework for fancies. You are mine, and I am going to be always
Yours,
Carl.

September 2, 1915

Washington D.C.
September 5, 1915

Dear Carl,

I am beginning the day with this note to you. Yours was truly welcome but it makes me feel anxious to see you soon. Of course I did not need a letter to tell me that you are big and sincere. To have had my life touched by yours will always prove a blessing.

You have heard the worst. There is nothing else <u>serious</u> to say. My hesitancy was due to a lack of courage to say that white is white. There are some very ordinary things that one finds a little difficulty in speaking about. I do realize that I've given you the blackest possible picture. But I don't regret it since God has been my refuge all through the <u>dark</u> period, I find it easy to say now, "Into Thy hands I commend my spirit." I have been told by someone whose opinion I usually value that in his opinion I've done a very unnecessary thing. That he wouldn't find another <u>sensible</u> person who would do the same thing. That seems strange to me, but can it be possible that love is anything but protective? Is it anything but genuine? Or is it that folks are not acquainted with it? Well, I still hold that I was right. If you were afraid, I feel that I could start again and, in course of time, regain myself. A struggle? Why of course, but I'm used to struggles. Every accomplishment, every success that I've known indicates struggle. For <u>myself</u> I have never or never intend to give a thought to the disagreed fact. It never crosses my mind. We look <u>back</u> and see no such conditions but find causes easily in the particular cases. We are proud of the fact that we can trace back our ancestry as a strong type. In my branch, something snapped. Hereditary? No, but acquired. Nature asserting itself for excesses in sacrifices, excesses in other ways which inevitably undermine health. It's an old story: the guiding hand of the home pays for the sacrifices made to protect its own, the tie gone each drifts into his own way. We look back and see what might have been. But after all, who knows?

I met Coach and Mr. Adams on the street Friday evening. They informed me that they had been to call on me. No one was home so I am compelled to believe that.

It's a wonder you are not coming over to the Tournament. Folks are beginning to get home and the city is taking on a business air.

It looks as though this is going to be a warm clear day. Shall probably go to church. Hope to see you very soon.

Sincerely, Vashti

"I Loved You Before I Told You"

Carl J. Murphy
Howard University
Washington, D.C.

Dear Vashti,

I awaited the outcome of James' conference with the president at Noon on Monday before coming over. President Newman assures him of the appointment so that we who have done high school and university together now teach the same subject side by side on the Hill. I am wondering can this be the climax of our mutual admiration society that has lasted now eleven years, or is something more to come. At any rate, it tempts one to believe in astrology --- we were born on the same day.

Dem Glücklichen schlägt keine Stunde says Schillers' Thekla to Max. The realization of the truth of this came first when I left you Sunday. Don't you see you have got to have strength when I have not, and insist that we finish our conversation the next time. Let's be sensible really after vacation.

When I asked you to be frank, brutally frank, even in my last letter, I did not have in mind the point under discussion alone, but all the points in our relations that are to be. That you are outspoken most times I have learned and I mentioned the incident that developed in my mind Vashti, individual, and not of Vashti, student. I believe I liked that better than anything you did the whole year. Sunday you drew a line between modesty or convention and frankness. I am afraid I know very little about conventions of many kinds, and expect that it's rather late to change --- unless you feel that it must be otherwise. They appear to have been invented to make types of us --- building a wall around the real self until love makes clear what is hidden there. We are tearing down now --- we have agreed we don't need this wall – so that when you put up a barrier, you make me feel I am suffering for sins committed.

I'm thinking do you know how little prepared I am to ask you to marry me now. Was this what occasioned your surprise when I did ask you? I insist you know, that you knew I loved you before I told you. Yet I felt I had to say both of them at once. I might have misused the second expression but never the first one. In saying it the first time, there was joy in an earnestness that I hope you too felt. Please be always as now, my angel of goodness.

Yours, Carl

September 14, 1915

Washington, D.C.

September 15, 1915

Dear Carl,

I was really glad to hear of James' good fortune and certainly rejoice with you both. There surely is some strange power behind the destinies of you two. No one hopes more than I that nothing will ever happen to block both your careers so promisingly begun. Your star has at least been a lucky one so far. A real mutual admiration society is a thing of joy to behold. May God bless you and make the year 1915-16 the most successful you've ever known.

At last I finished "Queed" but not until I had received a card from the library telling of its being due. The last chapters were most interesting. Professor Nicolonious alias Mr. Surface proves to be Queed's own father. Of course knowing this Queed cannot expose him but he endeavors to induce his father to return the money (the interest from which they lived on) he had managed to conceal and save from the State, to Sharlee. (This an intermediary which meant secrecy.) From the stormy interview which they held over the matter the father received a shock from which he never recovered. After his death the boy offers the return of every cent to Sharlee through their respective lawyers but she refuses to touch it.

If you remember, the "Post" of which Mr. Gardiner and Queed are Editor and Associate Editor, is making a strong plea in their editorials to force the legislature to pass a Reformatory Bill in which Miss Sharlee Weyland is deeply interested. Queed has written all of the articles and spun public opinion to his side. There is only one more needed, which he writes with a strong and masterful appeal.

Before it goes to press a political boss who knows of Gardiner's vanity and his desire to eventually be named for Mayor, convinces Gardiner that if he permits the paper to at this last stroke to plead for the Reformatory it will kill the party and his own chances. He believingly, refuses to print Queed's article, writing one himself which is quoted in the Legislature and kills the Reformatory Bill. Needless to say how Sharlee feels. She believes of course that Queed has turned traitor and turns her back on him. Gardiner having decided to ask her to marry him, seeing her deep resentment is too cowardly to state the truth. Queed quits his job for the paper and finds after the death of his father that he has made many friends.

Later Sharlee learns the truth; Gardiner falls in her sight while Queed gains her love. They decide to found a Reformatory with the money they both refuse to use for personal use, and name it, by her request, the Henry G. Surface Jr. Home, Queed having taken his rightful name. I enjoyed it;

the outcome immensely and think I'd like very much to know personally the new-made Queed.

Washingtonians are still sweltering but praying school teachers hope for an early relief.

I agree with you, Carl, and hope that from now on I shall really at all times, be able to think soberly and act sensibly. I really have no regrets, for I know my thoughts and actions have been spontaneous, dictated, though, solely by the heart. "More head" is a sensible cry. I can't close without making you see that I appreciate the highest possible tribute you have paid me by asking me to be your wife. There were no two things actually said. Had you said either one, according to my idea, it would have implied the other.

As to unpreparedness that means nothing. Rather it is a blessing. It enables me to pursue without protest things it will please me to pursue. It was dread of a possible protest which frightened me out of reason. Your surmise that I doubted your sincerity shocked. No one knowing you could do that. Because I have faith in you I would hate to thwart your plans. Yet I knew well, that reason demanded of me, if you were working in the now, no other step. That I pained you by my awkward way of making you see, I knew and regretted. It was untimely, and I should have known that it is sufficient to love and all other things will work themselves out. Isn't Schillers' Thekla's remark applicable here too?

To continue to be your companion is the sincere wish of Vashti

The Wedding

The Wedding

> 1415 Corcoran Street, N.W.
> June 14, 1916.
>
> Dear Prof. Murphy:
>
> Your note has been received. I shall be glad to officiate at your marriage at the time and place named in your note. You are getting one of the very nicest of all of our girls. Vashti is pure gold. My earnest prayer is that every blessing may attend you both.
>
> Very truly yours,
> Francis J. Grimke

Rev. Francis J. Grimke's letter agreeing to officiate Carl Murphy and Vashti Turley's wedding.

Rev. Grimke was an American Presbyterian minister in Washington, DC who was prominent in working for equal rights for African Americans. He was active in the Niagara Movement and helped found the National Association for the Advancement of Colored People (NAACP) in 1909.

Wikipedia.com

Mr. and Mrs. Guy B. Booth

announce the marriage of

their cousin

Lula Vashti Turley

to

Mr. Carl James Murphy

of Baltimore, Maryland

Tuesday, June twentieth

nineteen sixteen

At the Parsonage of the

Fifteenth Street Presbyterian Church

The Reverend Francis J. Grimke officiating

At Home
After September fifteenth
Montgomery Avenue
Takoma Park, Maryland

Official Wedding Invitation of Vashti Turley and Carl Murphy

Principles of Courtship

Courtship |ˈkôrtˌSHip| noun
A period during which a couple develops a romantic relationship, esp. with a view to marriage.

Up until the time I was 13, I visited my grandparents weekly. I fondly remember how respectful they were of one another, how they never seemed to compete with each other and how they truly enjoyed being in each other's company. If they ever uttered a harsh word to one another, shrugged a shoulder or rolled an eye, it was never in the presence of "the children". Their steadfastness and deep love for one another gave me a clear picture of the kind of marriage I wanted and I thank God for my husband and our 40 plus year marriage. I also thank my grandparents for leaving a written record of their "hook up".

Carl and Vashti Murphy's relationship was indeed "no ordinary hook up". It was built on a solid foundation of mutual interest, trust, respect and love. Their love letters, in addition to offering several principles of courtship, support my doctoral dissertation which concluded that there is a positive correlation between healthy, long-lasting marriages and solid premarital preparation. Although my grandparents' premarital preparation was not formally prescribed, it nonetheless resulted in a courtship that delved deeply into their beliefs, their likes and dislikes, their concerns, their habits and hobbies before they said, "I do".

From their love letters, my research and my own experiences, I offer the following *principles of courtship*:

1. Respect each other's opinions and learn how to disagree without being disagreeable.

2. Develop and pursue your own individual interests along with those you develop as a couple. Have fun together!

3. Openly discuss important issues, such as: sexual needs, finances, and family background (especially health histories).
4. Celebrate each other's milestones and accomplishments.
5. Agree on whether or not to have children and child rearing practices, in advance of your marriage.
6. Wait for the spouse God has for you. Don't rush into marriage; take time and pray before giving your answer. It's better to say, "no" or "not now", until you are 100 percent sure.
7. Remember that age and maturity are not synonymous. Don't be intimidated by an age difference.
8. Make sure you understand and are accepting of each other's faith traditions.
9. Write down your thoughts, your hopes, and your dreams for your life together. Leave a written and pictorial record for the next generation.
10. Be willing to listen to and discuss your spouse's political, social, civic and religious viewpoints – even when they are different from yours. Different does not mean deficient.
11. Begin with the end in mind understanding that marriage is a lifetime commitment; a marathon, not a sprint.
12. Pray for your spouse and your marriage daily. Ask God to mold your relationship into one that is pleasing to Him.

"Therefore a man shall leave his father and mother and be joined to his wife, and they shall become one flesh."
(Genesis 2:24, New King James Version)

ABOUT VASHTI TURLEY MURPHY

July 26, 1949

Mrs. Esther Popel Shaw
1111 Columbia Road, N.W.
Washington, D.C.

Dear Mrs. Shaw:

I see your note to the Mrs. asking why she is too modest to send you biographical data.

My experience tells me you may not get what you are seeking from The Lady herself, and I wonder if you should like these few words from me.

I do not know all the answers, but she is a very marvelous person, and after living with her for 33 years and wanting to a year before that, you ladies might accept a profile instead of a full length portrait done by herself.

She was born Lula Vashti Turley something over a half century ago in the capital of the nation. Her dad was a Turley and her mother a Francis. Her parents were married quite young and to their house came four children – Harry, Estelle, Chester and Vashti.

Father Turley was a clerk in the Pension Bureau handling checks for Civil War Veterans on work days. Sundays he was choirmaster of Plymouth Congregational Church and any night the neighborhood or glee club or choir members were in the Turley living room where Father Ham (Hamilcar) Turley presided at the piano and added his tenor to the community sing. Now and then the concert turned instrumental and the crowd brought out their mandolins and guitars.

In the afternoons, the house was full of children – the Turleys and their schoolmates. Vashti was the youngest. As was quite proper, she looked up to her elders. She will always remember the day her brother Chester left home wearing the uniform and shiny shoulder bars of a cadet lieutenant in Dunbar High School. She had never seen anything so magnificent. Adoringly she followed him out the front door and down the street. "You just can't walk behind me, "Chester admonished. "Everybody will know I have just been commissioned and am wearing a new uniform." Estelle was expert with needle and thread. She did the prettiest things with goods and patterns. Vashti could only sit and admire Estelle just as she followed behind Chester.

Like all children, Vashti changed into a young woman. She attended Dunbar High in the days when Mary Europe taught music and Miner Normal when Lucy Moten was principal. Normal School students were taught correct posture when standing or sitting. In chapel you sat stiffly erect. As the speaker of the day arose to speak you leaned forward slightly as evidence that you were attentive. The job of school teacher was to be taken seriously and you worked at the acquisition of poise, dignity, severity in dress and perfection in speech. Next came graduation and an appointment as teacher in Washington elementary schools.

A dutiful child took her first monthly check and gave it to a proud father. It thrilled him to no end. He fondled it carefully, looked at it and noted that she had endorsed it to him. And then he handed it back to her to keep—the first real money she had ever earned.

Howard University opened its classes to Washington school teachers. A degree then, as now, meant promotion and more pay. In addition, teachers were permitted to hold classes mornings or evenings and spend the other half day in college. You kept your job and earned your degree in four years. It was double work, but when you are young and ambitious you do not mind it too much.

This is where I came in. We met in my German classes. After her graduation, I received an invitation to call. Thereafter, whenever I could get her to accept, there were dates in which she met younger members of the Howard faculty: James H.N. Waring, Jr., now principal of Downingtown (Pa.) Industrial School; Dr. Charles Wesley, now president of Wilberforce; the late Ernest Marshall, a Kansas City physician, and the late Dr. Numa P.G. Adams, dean of Howard Medical School.

One Tuesday night in August, I asked her the S64 question. She would have to think it over, she said. By Thursday, her mind was made up, and she wrote her answer. It was <u>yes.</u>

We were married a year later, and found a $25 a month apartment and set up housekeeping. There was my pay of $72.50 a month, so we had $47.50 left for clothes, food and children. The latter came like steps—one approximately every two years. The third and fourth were twins. Finally, the total was five.

All of them are girls. Grown up now, they are married. The big house is deserted save for weekends and the summer months when the five come home with their husbands and ten grandchildren. So we have a nursery again filled up with balls, bats, wagons, skates, bassinets and cribs.

Four of our daughters are Deltas. Three of them were initiated at Wisconsin while attending the school of journalism there. The fourth was made at Howard University where her mother participated in the initiation.

The place we call home has albums of love letters, snapshots and pictures of birthday parties, weddings, babies, family gatherings and all the events that families like to treasure in their hearts. All of these scenes revolved these thirty years around the central figure of the household.

Hers is a great storehouse of sweetness and light for her own and for others. The Ancient Jews had a word for it. They said, "The dear God could not be everywhere, so He created mothers."

Very truly yours,
Carl Murphy

ABOUT CARL MURPHY

Dr. Carl James Greenbury Murphy was born in Baltimore, Maryland on January 17, 1889. He was the son of John Henry Murphy Sr. (1841-1922) and Martha Elizabeth Howard Murphy (1846-1915). His father, a former slave in Montgomery County who served in the Union Army and won his freedom, went on to found the Baltimore AFRO-American Newspaper in 1892.

Murphy was graduated from the Frederick Douglass High School in Baltimore and received his B.A. from Howard University in 1911 and a M.A. from Harvard University in 1913. In the summer of 1913, he attended the Friedrich Schiller University in Jena, Germany. He returned to Howard University that year as an instructor in German and in 1918 he became head of the school's German department. In 1948, he received an honorary doctorate from Lincoln University in Philadelphia. He also received honorary doctorates from Wilberforce University in 1960, and Morgan State University (posthumously) at its Founders' Day in 2014. Murphy was a lifelong member of the Alpha Phi Alpha Fraternity, Inc. and served as Editor-in-Chief of its magazine, *The Sphinx*, from 1918-1922.

Murphy gave up teaching and joined the AFRO-American Newspaper owned by his father to become its editor in the summer of 1918. Murphy immersed himself in his new career, learning all aspects of the newspaper business. His father died in 1922 and he was elected by his family to assume the role of publisher and chief editor of the newspaper, a position he would hold for the next 49 years.

The AFRO-American, under Murphy's leadership, became one of the largest circulating, most influential and most financially successful African American newspapers in the country. He greatly expanded the distribution area of the newspaper and produced a national edition as well as editions in Philadelphia, Richmond, Newark (N.J.) and the District of Columbia. He hired the best writers, artists and intellectuals and sent his reporters around the globe. During World War II, the AFRO's reporters were dispatched to cover African-American soldiers abroad. In 2015, Murphy was posthumously inducted into the Hall of Fame of the MDDC Press Association.

A vigorous civil rights crusader, the paper's headlines and editorials fought a continual battle against segregation. Murphy became chairman of the legal defense committee of the NAACP in 1935. He gave his time, talent and financial resources to this cause. He worked with Charles Houston and Thurgood Marshall on desegregating public schools and colleges -- from the University of Maryland starting with the Donald Murray case in 1935 to all public schools with the 1954 Brown v. Board of Education decision. He worked to desegregate restaurants, theaters, department stores, the armed forces and anywhere else where segregation existed. Murphy was also a strong foe of capital punishment. The NAACP awarded him the Spingarn Medal in 1955.

Murphy, the first African American chair of Morgan State University's (then College) Board of Regents, is credited with being the chief architect of its early expansion plans. He was a charter member of Morgan's board (1939-1953) and served as its vice chairman for 10 years, before being elected chair in in 1953. The University's Fine Arts Building is named in his honor.

He and his wife, Lula Vashti Turley Murphy, had five daughters: Martha Elizabeth Murphy Moss (1917-1998); Ida Murphy Peters (1918-1996); twins, Vashti Murphy Matthews (1921-1981) and Carlita Murphy Jones (1921-2006); and Frances L. Murphy, II (1922-2007). The Murphy Family attended Bethel A.M.E. and St. James Episcopal Churches in Baltimore, Maryland.

About Carl Murphy

Carl Murphy often quoted his father as saying, "I measure a newspaper not in buildings, equipment and employees. Those are the trimmings. A newspaper succeeds because its management believes in itself, in God and in the present generation."

Murphy died in Baltimore on February 25, 1967.

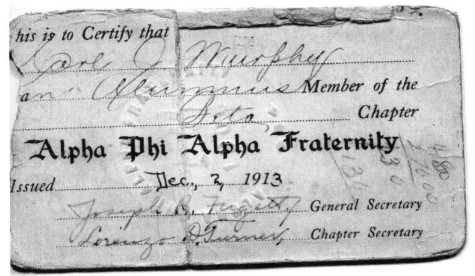

Pictured: Carl Murphy's Alpha Phi Alpha membership card

Grandchildren Remembrances

Three Generations of the Murphy Family - November 1952.
Front row: Robert Murphy Matthews, Sr., John Aaron Murphy Jones, Leeland Anthony Murphy Jones, Yvonne "Bonnie" Matthews Butler*, Frances Murphy Wood Draper, Martha Elizabeth Murphy Matthews Schuler, James Edward Wood, Jr., Vashti Murphy Smith McKenzie, Marie Murphy Phillips Braxton

Middle Row*: Vashti Murphy Matthews, Frances L. Murphy *(Wood)*, II, Carlita Murphy Jones, Vashti Turley Murphy, Carl J. Murphy, Ida Murphy Smith Peters, Elizabeth Murphy *(Phillips)* Moss

Back Row: Robert W. Matthews*, Sr., James Edward Wood, Sr. (Biddy)*, S. Edward Smith*, Carl Edward Murphy Smith

Seven more grandchildren were born between 1953 and 1958: Rodger Murphy Matthews, Benjamin Murphy Phillips, IV, Susan Murphy Wood Barnes, Rachael Murphy Phillips Humphrey, Carlita Candace Murphy Jones Perkins* and Carl Chester Matthews.

*Deceased

Carl and Vashti Turley Murphy had five daughters (Elizabeth, Ida, Carlita, Vashti and Frances); 8 grandsons and 8 granddaughters. Below are remembrances from three of the Murphy Grands:

"My earliest memories are at about 5 years old. I spent many days sleeping on the 3rd floor. They were not demonstrative at all. They were subtle. He would give a soft gentle whistle and she would appear. She protected his privacy particularly when writing editorials on Sunday evening. They reflected class and restraint in everything. They never stepped into each others' roles."

Carl E. Smith
Son of Ida Murphy Peters

"Memories of My Grandparents:
How well I remember as a child and early adolescent seeing the twinkle in the eyes of my Grandparents Murphy whenever they were in each other's presence. They truly were lovebirds! Grandmother Murphy had a beautiful voice and, it seemed, was always singing. Grandfather Murphy would hum or sing along. I shall never forget how they would hold hands when strolling in their beautifully landscaped gardens, forever smiling. Theirs was a genuine love story."

Rev. Dr. Marie Murphy Phillips Braxton
Daughter of Elizabeth "Bettye" Murphy Moss

"Grandmother and Grandfather Murphy always seemed to complement each other. It was clear that Grandmother ran the house, which is where I spent my most time with them. Structure was in place, provided for the grandchildren, and seemingly for every other family member, too. My Grandparents worked fluidly as a team, hosting Christmas breakfast, weekday dinners, weddings and funerals at the house that Grandfather built.

They sat together, laughed together and always seemed completely comfortable in each other's space. And (there was) always the commemorative photo, to memorialize the gathering of family and to signal to us that it was time to go. Looking back on those photos I see their solidarity and feel today their unfaltering commitment to one another. For we are the family that their love has built. A true blessing."

James E. Wood, Jr. MD
Son of Frances "Frankie" L. Murphy, II
and brother of the author

ABOUT THE AUTHOR

Rev. Dr. Frances Murphy Draper (Pastor Toni) is a native of Baltimore, MD, and holds several earned degrees including master's degrees in Education (Johns Hopkins University), Business Administration (University of Baltimore), and Pastoral Counseling (Loyola University Maryland). In 2006, she received her doctor of ministry degree in preaching and leadership from the United Theological Seminary in Dayton, Ohio. Her dissertation title was "Relationship Theology: A Model for Producing Healthy Marriages in the African American Context". In 2014, she co-authored (with Dr. Pamela Love Manning) *Life Happens, But You Can Finish... The Trials, Triumphs and Truths of 12 Amazing Finishers!*

Dr. Draper is the visionary and founding pastor of the Freedom Temple AME Zion Church in Baltimore, and the immediate past president and treasurer of the AFRO-American Newspapers – a publication founded by her great grandfather in 1892.

Since 1995, Dr. Draper has been a gubernatorial appointee to the Morgan State University Board of Regents (her alma mater), where she serves as vice chair. She and her husband, André, have been married for more than 40 years and they have four children and 12 grandchildren.

Dr. Draper has been a member of Delta Sigma Theta Sorority, Inc. for nearly 50 years and is the granddaughter of Delta Co-founder, Vashti Turley Murphy.

To order additional copies of *No Ordinary Hook Up* or to request a book talk or presentation by Dr. Draper, please email murphyhookup@gmail.com. The book also is available on amazon.com.

Sampling of Original Letters

HOWARD UNIVERSITY
WASHINGTON, D. C.

Dear Miss Turley,

I have just come from a stormy interview with the director of the Hopkins Summer School. We were nearly to the point of saying "can't" and "can" to each other. He was obdurate, however I insisted, maintaining virtually that all men are not created equal, and they celebrate to today the anniversary of the ratification of the declaration of Independence, this afternoon with community singing and games, tonight with fireworks. For our people it seems they are putting it — better half a country than no native land. I can't feel they are right.

Doctor was kind enough to ask me back to camp today. I promised to think about it. Remembering your advice tho, I am sending Wesley back alone.

Your diary is in the post, without a four-leafed clover, with some music, which I trust you are going to like. "Dawn" seems a simple melody with much of its charm in the accompaniment. I believe we have heard it together. "For you alone" I did not select because Caruso is said to have sung it.

And now for Du Bois' "The Negro". Until now the critics have kept quiet. They appear to be waiting for some one to find something especially praise- or blameworthy before they begin a tirade. Dean Miller thinks the book a compilation of quoted facts and represents little that is original, admits tho the chapter on the "Slave Trade" to be the big part of the book. One does miss the kind of imagination in DuBois history that paints pictures; pictures like Green's description of Queen

HOWARD UNIVERSITY
WASHINGTON, D. C.

intensely human, undoubtedly not inherently backward. In the past century DuBois' summaries of causes and results of movements illuminates after fifty years of cant and hypocrisy: the civil war was fought to segregate slavery not to abolish it; the Negro's need of immediate education and his control of the government during reconstruction are first causes of the rise of the public school system in the South; present poverty of the Negro is due to the failure of the government to make some payment for 250 years of slavery and free labor. These things not in the common histories, he thinks worth knowing and strives to popularize by sending forth "The Negro" in a fifty cent edition.

The plan of the book is extremely simple. Africa is divided into five geographical sections and the history of each brought down to the present day,—this one half the book. The second half, but one chapter, deals with the Negro in the New World, beginning with the arrival of slaves and concluding with a forecast of the future. The one chapter connecting the Old and the New Worlds is the one I have mentioned — "The Trade in Men." This was the subject of his Doctor's thesis at Harvard and is characteristically DuBoisian in contrasts and vittiness. You can't help feeling with him the cruel inhumanity that devasted all Africa and carried away one hundred million as slaves. And we think that Europe too would have been a "dark continent" had she suffered likewise, and this he concludes went on for four hundred years, while Luther preached, Rophael painted and Milton wrote. "Such is the story of the rape of Ethiopia," who during four centuries "stretched forth her hands unto God."

You may recall that DuBois

is an A.O.H. man. He told us some six years ago that there are many facts in Negro history doomed to remain hidden unless we develop Negro historians. He seems to have realized that the best way to get a thing done - - - , above all things he emphasizes as he always does that this race is ancients of ancients, a fallen hero and not a swaddling infant.

Trust you had a "hang up" trip

Very truly,
Carl J Murphy

July 5, 1915.
Letter from Baltimore 1320 D. H Ave

Washington, D.C.,
July 6, 1915.

Dear Mr. Murphy,

I must admit that my first day home was made quite interesting, all due to you. I first read the comment on the diary. I reread parts of it (diary) and lived over some experiences. I had to agree with you about the Holy Grail paintings but confess that at the time I simply accepted the condition as a matter of course. Another confession is that I've forgot what Miss Lewis told me about the walk. I think it is something I must look up for myself. Please don't pass judgment.

The music is a real treat. I have enjoyed both pieces today.

[margin note: by Edwin Austin Abbey. Says: To picture are the religious one. Prophets etc.]

I really believe you chose "For You Alone" because of the simplicity of the cover and the "Birth of Morn" because of recent early rising. It matters not about the reason, I shall enjoy them both and try hard to play them well enough for you to recognize them when you come over.

After reading later in the day the summary of "The Negro" I couldn't forget, try as hard as I might my promise. So I shall try to summarize "Redder Blood" though I fear I shan't be as pleased with my result as I am with yours.

× × — ∧ × × × × — ∽

7/7/'45.

Last night I reached the above place and just couldn't exert will power sufficient to continue. It was due no doubt to the long ride — aftereffects.

"Redder Blood" is an interesting story in which the author takes an old theme and dares to prove his foreword "that neither custom nor convention nor law are great enough barriers to keep two persons apart (who love deeply)." His characterization of the American white man who talks about abiding by the "laws of nature, justice & God" when he really isn't called upon to do anything is good. His manners when he realizes his wife has Negro blood but unlike the "New Governor" his character is strong enough not to be ruled by convention. If only a white author would dare! Of course we recognize that, as the only true attitude and hope the day will soon come when it will be universal. The author attempts further on to break down another convention, but I failed to relish it. To me it is a touch that spoils the book. He makes the girl, Wanda, a suitor to the man Adrian. He places all of the initiative on her which to me weakens both of the characters. And yet that is what he starts out to prove. To the first case (race) I say "Amen", to the second "Here"!!! There is too much prominence given to this part of the story anyway. That is the way I felt at first but now this afterthought makes one see that the author has endowed the white woman with "redder blood" which compels her to act as did the white man and such a method was probably necessary. I started off to write as though you knew the story, which I suppose you do. In fear you don't here is a synopsis.

Mr. Birch, a prominent and wealthy young man, meets with an accident and is carried to a hospital. He falls in love with his nurse and marries her. Their years pass by happily and their son proves himself worthy of their love. All goes well until a new man servant comes into the house as chef. He turns out to be one more who knows Mrs. Birch life history. She is of Negro decent. He tries to force her away with him and threatens to expose her. He uses many methods to get her away from her home but each time is thwarted. One morning her husband and son return home and surprise the man forcibly seizing Mrs. Birch. It is then that her husband learns the truth. He leaves home quietly, not intending that anyone shall know that he has left for good.

The son who is twenty-two and engaged immediately hastens to break his engagement; but the girl after her first display of anger and disgust decides that color is no barrier. Later the father returns for the same reason.

The author touches many social questions and sets forth an ideal point of view on some.

— Finis —

Had a delightful time on the Bay. The water was fine and there was quite an agreeable bunch of people. Unfortunately, we had tire trouble both ways. Otherwise the ride was lovely. He went through Baltimore going over but came back by Marlborough which is a more delightful and shorter ride.

If one could just chase away the mosquitoes, all would be well.

I tried to learn to take a stroke in the water but, alas, I always went to the bottom, until I finally gave up in disgust.

Went out this morning for a game of tennis. Had a nice game but no "pepper."

I fully appreciated how you must have felt after your recent interview, but at any rate I'll wager you gave him just a little food for thought. I suppose after all, we've got hope that something *must* happen soon. I'm afraid I regret giving that unasked for advice but will know better in the future.

Sincerely,

P. Vashti Turley.

The sweater was a necessity and don't know how I would have got on without it. *Thanks* again.

Sampling of Original Letters

CARL J. MURPHY
HOWARD UNIVERSITY
WASHINGTON, D. C.

Final letter
rewritten & sent
Sept 2
#1

Dear Vashti,

Do you remember you wanted to write some things rather than say them and that just as before I urged them now. You were right a second time. We could assure ourselves of either that only by waiting and thinking them. The new experience of finding you instantly overwhelmed anything that suggested a closing of the temple doors. Sensible now, but not then

CARL J. MURPHY
HOWARD UNIVERSITY
WASHINGTON, D. C.

8412
#2

was your idea of counting the cost before we became too happy.

"If one would only plan these things like he plans his work" — on the back of your last letter I wrote the two words health and income. These two things we were going to talk about in our three days. I did not know how hard it should be to bring such material things into our new world. I know now I did not want to. We did not finish the first.

CARL J. MURPHY
HOWARD UNIVERSITY
WASHINGTON, D. C.

Sept 2
#4

consider what has been or what will be. Like the first couple we start with ourselves. Of our own strength and will we may live, nor allow spectres of the past and future to frighten us. This is the theory of our family physician – for intelligent people there is no danger. It remains for us not to think that we are beginning with a handicap or that either of us concedes something here. Believe rather, that your self-sufficiency begins here, working as in all other things,

---

CARL J. MURPHY
HOWARD UNIVERSITY
WASHINGTON, D. C.

Sept 2
#3

Are we modern, you have asked? I am not if it means I shall give you up because of the untimely death of the others in your family. You have not told me about all of them yet, not that it can change the complexion of affairs do I ask it, but I feel that you want me to know. Today folk place emphasis, over emphasis – on the duty parents owe to their children that are to be. I believe we owe as much to ourselves. If we, both of us, are physically and mentally sound we need not

Sampling of Original Letters

CARL J. MURPHY
HOWARD UNIVERSITY
WASHINGTON, D. C.

SM 2 #5

whereof I love you.
I comprehend what it means to go over this with someone outside your immediate family. Churchill tho, was not wrong in his view that sacredness attaches itself more to mutual consent than to a ceremony. The first is the union of spirits and the second but the garment of custom. And this thing lets him as always be frank, brutally frank if necessary. Doubts too easily form a framework for fancies. You are mine and I am going to be always your Carl.

Baltimore, Md.
September 2, 1916

Washington, D.C.,
Sept. 5, 1915.

Dear Carl,

I am beginning the day with this note to you. Yours was truly welcome but it makes me feel anxious to see you soon. Of course it did not need a letter to tell me that you are big and sincere. To have my life touched by yours will always prove a blessing.

You have heard the worst. There is nothing serious to say. My hesitancy was due to a lack of courage to say that white is white. There are some very ordinary things that we find a little difficulty in speaking about. I do realize that I've given you the blackest possible picture. But I don't regret it. Since God has been my refuge all through the dark period, I find it easy to say now

"Thy hands I commend my spirit."
I have been told by some one whose opinion I usually value, that in his opinion I've done a very unnecessary thing. That he wouldn't find another sensible person who would do the same thing. That seems strange to me, but, can it be possible that love is anything but protective? Is it anything but genuine? Or is it that folks are not acquainted with it? Well, I still hold that I was right. If you were afraid, I feel that I could start again and, in course of time, regain myself. A struggle? I think of course, but I'm used to struggles. Every accomplishment, every success that I've known indicates struggle. For myself I have never or never intend to give a thought to the disagreeable fact. It never crosses my mind. He looks back and see no such conditions but find causes easily in the particular cases. We are proud of the fact that

can trace back our ancestry as a strong type. In my branch something snapped. Hereditary? No, but acquired. Nature asserting itself for excesses in sacrifices, excesses in other ways which inevitably undermine health. It's an old story; the guiding hand of the home pays for the sacrifices made to protect its own; the tie gone, each drifts into his own way. We look back and see what might have been. But after all, who knows?

I met Coach and Mr. Adams on the street Friday evening. They informed me that they had been to call on me. No one was home so I am compelled to believe that.

It's a wonder you are not coming over to the Tournament. Folks are beginning to get home and the city is taking on its business air.

It looks as though this is going to be a warm clear day. Shall probably go to

Sampling of Original Letters 103

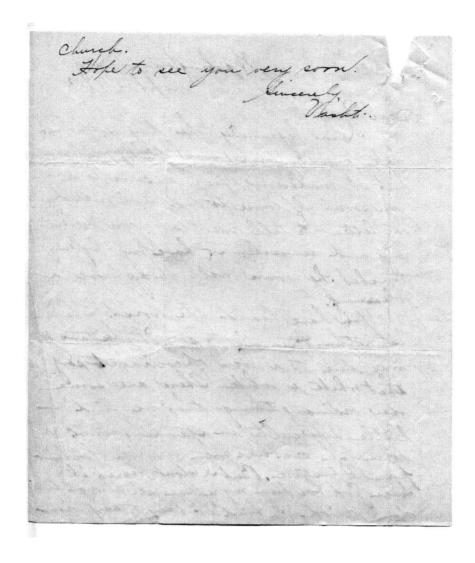

Church.
Hope to see you very soon.
Sincerely,
Vasht.

CARL J. MURPHY
HOWARD UNIVERSITY
WASHINGTON, D. C.

Dear Vashti,

I awaited the outcome of Jamie's conference with the president at noon on Monday before coming over. President Newman assures him of an appointment so that we who have done high school and university together now teach the same subject side by side on the Hill. I am wondering can this be the climax of our mutual admiration society, that has lasted now eleven years, or is something more to come. At any rate it tempts one to believe in astrology; we were born on the same day.

CARL J. MURPHY
HOWARD UNIVERSITY
WASHINGTON, D. C.

„Dem Glücklichen schlägt keine Stunde" says Schiller's Thekla to Max. The realization of the truth of this came first when I left you Sunday. Don't you see, you have got to have strength when I have not, and insist that we finish our conversation the next time. Let's be sensible really after vacation.

When I asked you to be frank, brutally frank even, in my last letter, I did not have in mind the point under discussion alone, but all the points in our relations that are to be. That you are outspoken sometimes I have learned and I mentioned the incident that developed in my mind

CARL J. MURPHY
HOWARD UNIVERSITY
WASHINGTON, D. C.

Vashti individual out of Vashti student. I believe I liked that better than anything you did the whole year. Sunday you drew a line between modesty & convention and frankness. I am afraid I know very little about conventions of many kinds, and regret that it is rather late to change,—unless you feel that it must be otherwise. They appear to have been invented to make types of us—building a wall around the real self until love makes clear what is hidden there. We are tearing down now—we have agreed we don't need the wall—so that when you put up a barrier, you make me feel I am suffering

---

CARL J. MURPHY
HOWARD UNIVERSITY
WASHINGTON, D. C.

for some committed.
    I'm thinking — do you know how little prepared I am to ask you to marry me now. Was this what occasioned your surprise when I did ask you? I meant, you know, that you knew I loved you before I told you. Yet I felt I had to say both of them at once. I might have misused the second expression but never the first one. I'm saying it the first time there was joy in an earnestness that I hope you too felt. Please be always as now my angel of goodness.
                        your
                        Carl

September 14, 1915.

Washington, D.C.,
Sept. 15, 1915.

Dear Carl,

I was really glad to hear of Jane's good fortune, and certainly rejoice with you both. There surely is some strange power behind the destinies of you two. No one hopes more than I that nothing will ever happen to block your careers so promisingly begun. Your star has at least been a lucky one so far. A real mutual admiration society is a thing of joy to behold. May God bless you and make the year 1915-16 the most successful you've ever known.

At last I finished "Queed" but not until I had received a card from the Library telling of its being due. The last chapters were most interesting. Professor Nicolovius alias Mr. Surface proves to be Queed's own father. Queed knowing this Queed cannot expose him but he endeavors to induce his father to return the money (the interest from which they lived on)

he had managed² to conceal and save
from the state, (this an intermediary which meant nothing) to Sharlee. From the
stormy interview which they held over
the matter the father received a shock
from which he never recovered. After
his death the boy offers the return
of every cent to Sharlee through their
respective lawyers, but she refuses to
touch it.

If you remember, the "Post" of which
Mr. Gardiner & Queed are Editor and
Associate Editor, is making a strong
plea in their editorials to force the
legislature to pass a Reformatory Bill
in which Miss Sharlee Weyland is deeply
interested. Queed has written all of the
articles and spun public opinion to
his side. There is only one more
needed, which he writes with a strong
and masterful appeal.

Before it goes to press a political
boss who knows of Gardiner's vanity
and his desire to eventually be named

3.

for Mayor, convinces Gardiner that if he permits the paper to at this last stroke to plead for the Reformatory it will kill the party and his own chances. He, believingly, refuses to print Queed's article, writing one himself which is quoted in the Legislature and kills the Reformatory Bill. Needless to say how Sharlee feels. She believes of course that Queed has turned traitor and turns her back on him. Gardiner having decided to ask her to marry him, seeing her deep resentment, is too cowardly to state the truth. Queed quits his job for the paper and finds after the death of his father that he has made many friends.

Later Sharlee learns the truth. Gardiner falls in her sight while Queed gains her love. They decide to found a Reformatory with the money they both refuse to use for personal use, and to name it, by her request, the Henry

Q. Surface Home, Queed having taken
his rightful name. I enjoyed it, the
outcome immensely, and think I'd like
very much to know personally the
new-made Queed.

Washingtonians are still sweltering but
praying school teachers hope for an
early relief.

I agree with you, Carl, and hope that
from now on I shall really, at all
times, be able to think soberly and act
sensibly. I really have no regrets, for I
know my thoughts and actions have
been spontaneous, dictated, though, solely
by the heart. "More head" is a sensible cry.

I can't close without making you see
that I appreciate the highest possible tribute
you have paid me by asking me to be your
wife. There were no two things actually
said either one, according to my idea, it
would have implied the other.

As to unpreparedness that means nothing.
Rather it is a blessing. It enables me
to pursue without protest things it will

please me to pursue.⁵· It was dread of a possible protest which frightened me out of reason. Your surmise that I doubted your sincerity shocked. No one knowing you could do that. Because I have faith in you I would hate to thwart your plans. Yet I knew well, that reason demanded of me, if you were working in the now, no other step. That I pained you by my awkward way of making you see, I knew and regretted. It was untimely, and I should have known that it is sufficient to love and all other things will work themselves out. Isn't Schiller Thekla's remark applicable here too.

To continue to be your companion is the sincere wish of Vaclt.

Sampling of Original Letters

Made in the USA
Columbia, SC
20 October 2017